HEAL THYSELF COOKBOOK

DIANE CICCONE

Introduction by
Queen Afua

*A Complete Guide
to Natural Living
through
Vegetarian Cooking
and
Holistic Juicing*

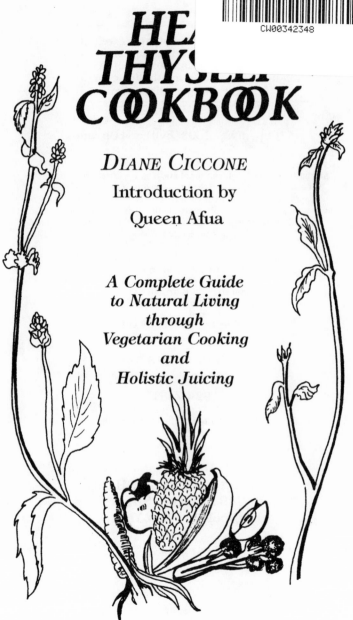

A&B BOOKS PUBLISHERS
Brooklyn, New York
11201

The Publisher wishes to thank the
Heal Thyself Organization
and *Natural Planetary Healers*
for reproduction of material
and
Shirley McRae for preliminary editing

ISBN 1-881316-07-6
LIBRARY OF CONGRESS CATALOG NUMBER

92-074511

manufactured in the United States

ooooo

A&B BOOKS PUBLISHERS
149 Lawrence Street
Brooklyn , New York
11201
(718) 596-3389

FIRST PRINTING 1992

SECOND PRINTING 1993

2 3 4 5 6 7 8 9 10 11 12

HEAL THYSELF COOKBOOK

NO DAIRY   NO EGGS   NO SALT

CONTENTS

Introduction

*I*N THESE CHALLENGING BUT POWERFUL times on this planet, where there is unrest, rampant dis-ease and suffering due to poor choices, we are never the less given a way out, a new opportunity. With making the best most productive choices we can experience health and wholeness in our lives. The Creator is ever present and supportive in our need to be well in Body, Mind & Soul. The Most High never fails to send us guides to aid us on our return back to our natural state of divinity, health, peace and wellness, after all it is our birthright to be well.

One of such guides is Diane Ciccone. Through her divine love and work with holistic foods and juices by way of the *"Heal Thyself Natural Living Cookbook"* we are given the opportunity to "Heal Thyself".

So much present day anger, stress and premature aging derives from our constant daily intake of fast foods, man-made processed foods and devitalized foods. On the other hand by consuming natural foods of fresh fruit, vegetables, whole grains, seeds, nuts and live juices, along with specific herbs and spices, we are able to experience joy, peace, harmony, longevity, vitality and a body free of dis-ease. For you see, "we truly are what we eat".

Once you taste these wonderful wholesome recipes born out of Diane Ciccone, on how to prepare God's foods naturally, observe how beautifully your life unfolds. The recipes contained within these pages are a traditional diet of fuller heavier meatless meals to simpler uncooked vegetarian meals. Remember less is better! You will find that the lighter simpler foods give you greater power and strength which in the end help you to manifest a more masterful productive life.

With Diane Ciccone's 22 years of consistent dedication and commitment to living a natural life style, living on the "Heal Thyself Path of Purification", coupled with her being from the first class to have graduated as a Certified Heal Thyself Professor of Purification, she unselfishly was lead to write and share this work of natural living so that we could have a Natural Living Dietary Guide to live intuned with nature, ourselves, our families, our neighbors and the universe.

The foundation of this work stems from the Heal Thyself Principle that your kitchen is your laboratory. The most crucial room within your home for restoring and purifying the body temple is non other than that knowledge that is contained with your "Kitchen Laboratory". From internalizing and incorporating these readings, you to will have the power to Heal Thyself.

QUEEN AFUA

Foreword

I HAVE BEEN A VEGETARIAN for over twenty years. During that time the most frequently asked questions, of me, were: "Isn't eating only vegetables boring?" and "I wouldn't know how to cook a vegetarian meal, how do you do it?". This book is designed to answer both questions and more.

The Heal Thyself Natural Living Center's philosophy is The key to good wholesome living is living a clean wholesome life. That begins with eating clean wholesome food.

This cookbook is dedicated and written for those who want to cook and eat clean wholesome food. All recipes are animal, sugar and salt free. Many are also oil free.

Although a vegetarian diet with a high percentage of live food is ideal, many of us for whatever reason cannot or do not eat that way on a consistent daily basis. This book has a variety of vegetarian recipes. If you are beginning on a vegetarian diet, many of the heavy "carbohydrate" recipes will make your transition from a meat based diet to a vegetable based diet easier. As you adjust to a vegetarian diet, you should use more

of the live foods and juice recipes in your meal planning. If you
have a high percentage of live food in your diet or are beyond a
"sophomore level" in Queen Afua's Natural Living Program
many of the "heavier" recipes which contain tofu, nuts, rice,
gravies or pasta may be too heavy and should not be eaten. In
many cases, the "heavier" vegetarian recipes can be adapted to
reflect a lighter more "live" diet. This cookbook keeps this in
mind. You will soon learn that a healthy wholesome diet can be
exciting, creative and fun.

ENJOY !

Acknowledgement

*I*GIVE THANKS AND PRAISES TO THE CREATOR, without whom none of this would have been possible.

I wish to thank Queen Afua for gently encouraging me to complete this project.

I thank my family, Daryl and Kali, for their patience, support and inspiration.

Thanks to the Professors of Purification for their recipes and the many other folks through the years.

Special thanks to Gloria for her beautiful illustrations. Many thanks to Shirley McRae my editor and friend.

Diane Ciccone

PREPARING YOUR KITCHEN

Many people who are making the transition to a natural living (vegetarian) diet are concerned about what they need in their kitchen. A well stocked natural living kitchen is not very different from any other kitchen. I have prepared a brief list of the types of items which are helpful in your preparation of a natural living meal.

POTS/PANS

Stainless steel or glass is preferable. Aluminum and teflon should be avoided. Medical studies have linked cooking in aluminum pots to Alzheimer's disease.

UTENSILS

A good set of knives is invaluable for cutting/slicing fruits and vegetables. Large wooden spoons are good for mixing. I prefer wood to plastic or metal spoons for mixing, however, they can be used. *A note about plastic:* we should all be ecologically conscience and cut back on our plastic use.

STORAGE CONTAINERS

Large glass mason jars are an excellent way to store your grains, flours and pastas. A bay leaf in each jar will help keep grains and flours from getting bugs. *A note about storing:* unless you use your flours and oils in a short period of time, they are better kept in the refrigerator to prevent rancidity.

FOOD PROCESSORS

Although this is an optional item, some recipes that require food to be chopped very fine are best prepared in a food processor. If you cook in large quantities food processors can cut down on preparation time. As you begin to eat more live foods a processor becomes invaluable.

BLENDERS

A must for every kitchen. Used in many beverage recipes.

JUICERS

A must for anyone on a natural living diet.

STEAMERS

There are electric, ceramic and metal steamers. Which steamer you choose depends on your budget. The least expensive is the metal steamer basket which is placed inside the cooking pot and covered.

PRESSURE COOKER/CROCK POT

This is optional. If your budget allows, go for it. The pressure cooker/crock pot cuts down on cooking times.

FOOD STOCK

SPICES

Powders are preferable to salts, i.e.., garlic, onion, celery powders. If needed, there are many salt substitutes on the market. Cayenne pepper is preferable to black pepper. Black pepper irritates the intestinal lining. Always buy nonirridated spices. They will be labeled and are generally found in health food stores.

SWEETENERS

Honey, maple syrup, brown rice syrup, molasses, barley malt and date sugar are excellent natural substitutes to sugar.

CONDIMENTS

A trip to your local health food store is highly recommended. You can substitute *ALL* your present condiments with ones that are sugar and salt free and do not have any animal products or by-products in them. The key to purchasing any product is to read the labels. Many products use the word "natural", but are still laden with sugar, salt and animal products or by-products.

SPROUTS

Can be purchased in grocery or health food stores. However, the cheapest way is to grow your own. An excellent resource book is Ann Wigmore's, "The Sprouting Book".

SOME ITEMS THAT YOU MANY WANT TO KEEP ON HAND

Liquid Lecithin & Granules
Egg Replacer
Wheat Germ
Flax Seeds
Psyllium Husks
Apple Cider Vinegar

Herbs - What you use depends on your own tastes. Herbs are a good source of seasoning as well as being good for you. Fresh herbs in your recipes give more flavor. Herbs are easy to grow, if you don't have a garden, plant in pots and put in a window.

Breakfast

1

*I*N OUR HOUSE, Sunday breakfast was a meal where no one was rushing to go anywhere and we could all eat together. My mother would fix pancakes, eggs, bacon, sausage or ham. Although the mealtime was special, the heavy starch and grease of the pork would leave my stomach in distress for the rest of the day. Many years later, I realized the importance of that first meal, break-fast, for it is the meal that can set the tone for the entire day.

The following recipes are "heavy" vegetarian meals. They are ideal if you are in a transition diet or to eat on that "special" and "rare occasion", not to be eaten more than once or twice a week. Those following the Natural Living Program should drink the pre-breakfast followed by a live juice or fresh fruit meal.

PREBREAKFAST DRINK

1 lemon, juiced
1 grapefruit, juiced
1 orange, juiced
8 - 16 oz. warm water

Mix all ingredients. NOTE: Do not eat for at least 1/2 hour.

FRENCH TOAST

Batter:
1 1/2 cups tofu
1 tsp. ground cinnamon
2 Tbs. real maple syrup
1/2 cup water or soy milk

Bread:
8 slices day-old whole grain bread

In a blender, blend all ingredients until smooth. Pour into a shallow dish.

Dip the bread in the batter, then fry on a hot griddle or skillet in butter or oil until golden brown on both sides. Alternative: Bake at 350 degrees on a well oiled pan until golden on each side.

BREAKFAST RICE PUDDING

1/2 cup cooked brown rice
1/2 cup milk (soy)
1/2 tsp. vanilla
1 Tbs. toasted wheat germ
2 Tbs. broken nuts or sunflower seeds
1 tsp. molasses
Cinnamon or Nutmeg (optional)

Combine all ingredients in a small saucepan. Gently cook, covered, for five minutes. Serve warm, with a sprinkle of cinnamon or grating of nutmeg, if desired.
This makes one serving.

SCRAMBLED TOFU

1lb. tofu, crumbled (squeeze out excess water)
1 small onion, chopped
1 small pepper, chopped
1/4 tsp. garlic powder
1/4 tsp. turmeric
1 tsp. nutritional yeast
Chopped Chives to taste

Saute onion and pepper in water. Add tofu, mash with a fork until completely crumbled, add remaining ingredients, mix well blending all flavors. This is done over a low flame.

MUESLI

4 oz. rolled oats
2 oz. figs, chopped
1 oz. hazelnuts, chopped
1/2 tsp. ground cinnamon
2 apples, grate just before serving

Place oats and figs in a bowl, add water just to cover. Leave overnight in covered bowl. Before serving add the remaining ingredients and mix well. Serve with soy milk or any nut milk.

CRUNCHY GRANOLA

Mix dry ingredients together:
4 cups rolled oats
1/2 cup coconut
3/4 cup slightly roasted nut (peanut or other)
1/2 cup pumpkin or sunflower seeds
Mix in separate bowl and add to dry ingredients:
3/4 Tbs. honey
1 Tbs. vanilla
1/4 cup oil

Mix together thoroughly and spread on shallow edged baking sheet. Bake at 300 for 45 minutes until light brown. Reduce heat to 225 and bake until dry. Stir occasionally while baking. Add 1/2 cup raisins or chopped nuts.

Appetizers
2

HOW MANY OF THOSE SOCIAL GATHERINGS have you gone to and the appetizers that you could possibly choose from were: chips, nuts, raw broccoli and carrots with a dip that you dare not ask the contents? Well, here are few suggestions for the hostess.

MARINATED MUSHROOMS

4 cups small fresh mushrooms (about 1 pound)
1 cup water
1/2 cup brown rice or apple cider vinegar
1 bay leaf
1 clove garlic, sliced or quartered
2 to 3 sprigs fresh basil
(or pinch dried basil)
2 to 3 sprigs fresh thyme or oregano(or
pinch dried thyme or oregano)
2 Tbs. olive oil, preferably Italian
2 Tbs. slivered scallion
1 Tbs. minced parsley
Parsley sprigs and strips of
fresh lemon peel for garnish

This appetizer requires only 10 minutes of preparation time. Let the mushrooms marinate at least 12 hours, but no longer than three days.

Wash mushrooms, trim stems, and place caps in a heatproof bowl. Set aside. Combine water, vinegar, bay leaf, garlic and herbs in a small saucepan. Bring mixture to a boil, simmer no more than 1 minute, add oil after removing from heat, and pour over mushrooms. Allow to cool, then cover bowl and refrigerate at least 12 hours before serving. Toss occasionally so mushrooms will marinate evenly.

To serve, drain mushrooms and remove bay leaf, garlic and herb sprigs. Toss mushrooms with slivered scallion and minced parsley. Place in a serving bowl and garnish with parsley sprigs and lemon peel.

Makes 4 cups- serves 32.

CARROT PATE

Carrot Mixture:
1 cup water
2 cups chopped carrots
1/4 tsp. dill weed
1/2 tsp. salt-free vegetable seasoning
1/2 tsp. vegetable protein powder
1/4 tsp. granulated garlic
2 1/2 tsp. nutritional yeast
3/4 tsp. granulated onion
Other:
2 Tbs. unroasted sesame seed oil
4 Tbs. finely-ground, whole wheat flour

Blend carrot mixture ingredients until smooth; pour into pot and simmer 10 minutes on top of stove.

Brown wheat flour in sesame oil, then add to hot carrot mixture to thicken.

Cool. Use as a spread, dip, or for canapes. **Note:** The oil is the smoothing element, which also keeps the pate moist.

CAULIFLOWER COUSCOUS PATE

4 cups steamed, well-done cauliflower pieces
4 cups steamed couscous,
prepared according to standard directions

Blend above ingredients, still hot,
in blender or food processor.

2 tsp. granulated garlic
1 1/2 tsp. onion powder
1/2 tsp. ground nutmeg
1/4 tsp. ground cayenne pepper

In a blender or food processor, combine all ingredients
with the couscous mixture and mix until smooth. Serve piping
hot. This recipe can also be used as an appetizer spread on
canapes or as a dip for crackers.

Yield: 6 cups.

STUFFED ENDIVE LEAVES

8 ounces fresh tofu
1/4 cup mellow white miso
2 Tbs. lemon juice or brown rice vinegar
2 Tbs. safflower or sesame oil
1 clove garlic, finely minced or pressed
3 Tbs. fresh minced onion (or 2 Tbs. dried onion)
1/2 cup minced red bell pepper
1/2 cup minced celery
20 Belgian endive leaves (separated from
two to three large Belgian endive)
20 sprigs watercress

Place tofu in boiling water to cover. Turn off heat, cover, let sit a few minutes, then place the tofu in cold water to cool. Remove tofu, wrap in cheesecloth or porous cotton, and gently squeeze out excess water.

Place tofu, miso, juice or vinegar, oil and garlic in a blender and blend until smooth. Stir in onion, pepper and celery. Let rest, refrigerated, at least 2 hours to allow flavors to heighten. The stuffing mixture can be made one or two days in advance if kept covered in the refrigerator.

At serving time, taste tofu mixture and adjust seasonings. Place a heaping teaspoon of tofu mixture on the lower third of each endive leaf. Tuck a sprig of watercress into the mixture so it rests on the endive leaf. Place the pieces on a platter in a fan shape, or other attractive arrangement.

Makes 20 appetizers.

STUFFED CELERY STICKS

1 mashed avocado, seasoned with lemon juice
1/8 teaspoon kelp
Celery stalks

Cut the celery in 5 inch lengths and fill with avocado.
Variations: Stuff celery with tofu eggless salad (pg.51);
carrot, olive or cauliflower pate (pg.20)

Beverages

3

WITH ALL THE "ARTIFICIAL" BEVERAGES on the market i.e.., soda, fruit punch, kool ades, etc.. I wanted to give some simple yet tasty alternatives. For those who can not live without milk, there are nut milks which are nutritious substitutes and can be substituted for cow's or goat's milk.

Enjoy, but remember drink fluids at least 1/2 to 1 hour before or after your meal, but *NEVER* during your meal.

RICE MILK

4 cups water
1 cup brown rice, cooked
1 tsp. vanilla (optional)

Blend ingredients in blender or food processor until smooth.
Refrigerate. Shake before using.

NUT & SEED MILK I

1/2 cup almonds
1/2 cup sesame seeds or cashews
1 quart water
2 Tbs. maple syrup

Blend ingredients until smooth.

COCONUT MILK

1 1/2 cups fresh coconut, shredded or grated
1 quart water
2 Tbs. sunflower oil

Blend ingredients until smooth.

**NOTE: USE ONLY RAW NUTS. ALL NUTS SHOULD BE
SOAKED IN WATER OVERNIGHT.**

COCONUT-ALMOND MILK

1/2 cup coconuts
1/2 cup almonds
5 dates
1 quart water

Blend ingredients until smooth.

BANANA SMOOTHIE

1 cup soy milk
1 cup ice
3 medium-size bananas
2 Tbs. honey

Blend ingredients until smooth.

COMFREY PINEAPPLE COOLER

2 cups pineapple juice
1 cup fresh comfrey leaves
1 sprig fresh mint
Handful of fresh parsley or watercress

Orange juice can be substituted for the pineapple juice.
Combine all ingredients in a blender and process until
smooth. **Serves 2**

MELON-ORANGE FRAPPE

2 cups fresh melon chunks
1 cup fresh orange juice
1 cup crushed ice

Blend all ingredients until smooth.
Serves 2

FRUIT n FLAX

1 Tbs. flax seed meal
6 ounces fruit juice
1 small banana
1 ice cube

Blend flax seed and juice. Let stand 10 minutes. Add banana and ice cube and blend until smooth.

HOT SPICED CIDER

1 gallon apple cider
2 oranges
2 lemons
8 whole cloves
1 stick cinnamon
1 tsp. whole allspice

Slice oranges and lemons, remove seeds. Cut slices in half (leave on rind). Put all ingredients in large pan; bring to boiling point, but do not boil. Serve piping hot. To reheat leftover cider, remove spices.

GRAPE SPRITZER

2 1/2 cups chilled white grape juice
1 1/2 cups chilled sparkling water
Lime or lemon wedges
Frozen green grapes
(optional garnish)

Choose elegant glasses. Fill each with 5 oz. grape juice and 3 oz. sparkling water. Add a small cluster of frozen green grapes and a slice of lime or lemon.

Serves 4

MINT COOLER

1/2 cup fresh mint leaves
1/2 cup natural lemonade
1/3 cup lime juice drink
4 or 6 ice cubes
1 slice of lime

Combine mint leaves, lemonade, lime juice drink and ice cubes in a blender and blend until smooth. Twist the lime slice and place on top. Serve immediately.

ORANGE MIST

1 cinnamon orange tea bag
1/3 cup boiling water
1/2 cup orange juice
4 to 6 ice cubes
1/4 cup sparkling water

Pour boiling water over the tea bag and steep for 5 minutes. Remove the tea bag. Put the tea, juice and ice cubes into a blender and blend until smooth. Add sparkling water and serve immediately.

TEA AND FRUIT POP

1/2 cup prepared herbal tea
1/2 cup carbonated fruit juice, such as
sparkling tangerine juice
Brown rice malt syrup, to taste

In a tall glass or pitcher, combine the tea, several ice cubes and the fruit juice of your choice. If desired, sweeten to taste with the brown rice syrup.

APPLE WHIZ

Add four bags of cinnamon tea to one quart unfiltered apple juice. Let sit for several hours. Refrigerate, serve over ice.

SUN TEA COCKTAILS

6 bags herbal tea or equivalent loose tea
2 cups water
Maple syrup to taste
2 cups ice cubes
2 cups chilled sparkling water

Prepare sun tea. Stir in maple syrup and add ice cubes. Stir until thoroughly chilled. Add sparkling water.

Serves 6

GINGER ALE

2 lemons
1 quart fresh water
1 cup fresh ginger root, peeled and chopped
1 quart sparkling water
Honey
Dash of cayenne pepper (optional)

Peel the lemons and cut the peels into thin strips. Place in a saucepan with ginger. Add four cups fresh water and bring to a boil. Cover and let steep for 10 minutes. Strain and add honey and juice of peeled lemon to taste. A pinch of cayenne pepper adds zip. Chill. To serve, add one part sparkling water to three parts ginger mix. Add ice.

Makes about 2 quarts. Serves 6 - 8

TROPICAL FRUIT TEA

2 quarts water
3 Tbs. hibiscus flowers
3 Tbs. mint leaves
3 Tbs. lemon grass
1/2 cup pineapple, chopped
2 oranges, sliced
1 papaya, slice
1 mango or other tropical fruit (optional)

Bring water to a boil, turn off the heat and add the hibiscus, mint and lemon grass. Let steep 20 minutes and strain. Put the fruits into a 2 quart jar and pour the tea over them. Refrigerate overnight.

ROOT BEER

1/2 cup each: cinnamon, sarsaparilla,
sassafras, wintergreen
1 quart water
1/2 cup honey
3 cups carbonated water

Simmer herbs in water for 10 minutes. Strain out herbs. Add honey and cool. Add carbonated water before serving.

HOT CAROB DRINK

1 1/2 cups soy milk
2 tsp. carob powder
1 tsp. honey
Dash of vanilla extract
1/2 tsp. cinnamon

Blend all ingredients and heat gently.
Serves 1

Live Juices
4

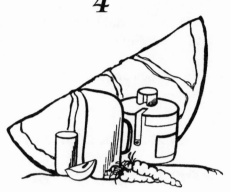

"LIVE JUICES" ARE THE JUICE of any fresh fruits or vegetables. By drinking "live juice" the body is able to assimilate and utilize the vitamins and minerals from the fruit or vegetable. This is beneficial whether you are healthy and using live juice as preventive maintenance or if you are on a program designed to help rid the body of dis-ease.

Live juices are essential to any fasting or natural living program. Live juice will provide you with the vitamins, minerals and amino acids needed to detoxify, build and repair your body. Please refer to Queen Afua's book, "Heal Thyself with Life and Longevity" for a complete discussion of the benefits of Juice Fasting.

A few "musts" when drinking live juices:

1.   Thoroughly wash and scrub the skins to remove all dirt. Use Dr. Bronner's soap or commercial washes—available in health food stores—to remove pesticides and chemical residue. For foods that have been waxed, cut off the skin before juicing. Whenever possible use organic fruits and vegetables.

2.   Any live juice must be consumed within 15 minutes. Virtually all the minerals and vitamins are lost through oxidation after 15 minutes.

3.   Fruit juice will detoxify and cleanse the body of accumulated waste. Vegetable juice will build and repair the body.

The following recipes are only a sample of the countless variations. Be creative!

"VEGETABLE JUICE COMBINATIONS"

CARROT GINGER ZING

5 carrots, cleaned and cut to fit in juicer
1/2" root of fresh ginger

Note: The "zing" can be modified by the amount of ginger used.

VEGGIE COCKTAIL

3 carrots
3 celery stalks

Wash and juice all ingredients.

SPRING SWEEP

5 carrots
1 beet

Wash and juice all ingredients.

CUCUMBER COOLER

2 cucumbers, peeled
1 carrot

Wash and juice all ingredients.

BLOOD SUGAR TONIC*

1 cup alfalfa sprouts
1 cup mung sprouts
1 cup lentil sprouts
2 kale leaves
1 cup Jerusalem artichokes
1 handful string beans
1 medium parsnip
1/2 cup fennel

Wash ingredients. Combine, juice and serve.
*Submitted by Ada Robinson, Professor of Purification and Assistant to Queen Afua.

CARROT/TURNIP

5 carrots
1 turnip

Wash and juice all ingredients.

CARROT/CABBAGE

5 carrots
1/2 head cabbage

Wash and juice all ingredients.

CARROT/STRING BEAN

5 carrots
1/2 cup of string beans

Wash and juice all ingredients.

CARROT/SPINACH

5 carrots
1 bunch of spinach

Wash and juice all ingredients.

GREEN DRINK

1/2 - 1 bunch parsley
2 - 3 sprigs watercress
2 - 3 leaves of kale
1/2 cucumber, (peeled, if waxed)

Wash and juice all ingredients.

"FRUIT JUICE COMBINATIONS"

PINEAPPLE SUPREME

2 rings of fresh pineapple
2 oranges, peeled

PINEAPPLE SUPREME PLUS

2 rings of fresh pineapple
2 oranges, peeled
1 large grapefruit, peeled

Peel and juice all ingredients.

CITRUS WAKE UP

1 large grapefruit
2 oranges
1 lemon

Peel and juice all ingredients.

NOTE: When peeling citrus fruits, be sure to keep the white pith on fruit. The beneficial nutrients are in the pith.

GRAPEFRUIT/ORANGE

2 grapefruits
1 orange

Peel and juice all ingredients.

CRANAPPLE

2 cups fresh cranberries
2 apples

Wash and juice all ingredients.

PEACH/STRAWBERRY

2 peaches
1 cup strawberries

Pit peaches, wash and juice all ingredients.

WATERMELON

2 slices of watermelon

Thoroughly wash and juice, include rind and seeds.

Salads/Dressings

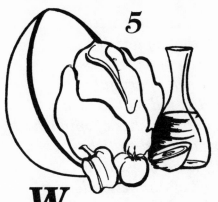

5

WE BSTER'S NINTH COLLEGIATE dictionary defined salads as : An oncongruous mixture : Hodgepodge.

Traditionally salads have been used as a side dish or appetizer. I assure you, the following recipes will open up the world of a meal in a salad and a salad in a meal.

SO YOU SAID
YOU WANTED A SALAD*

1 head Romaine lettuce
1 bunch of parsley
1 bunch of watercress
1 bunch of arugula
1 head of red leaf lettuce
1/2 pkg. or 2 bunches of spinach
10 grated red radishes
1/2 head of escarole
1/2 bunch of dandelion leaves
1/2 pkg. of clover sprouts
1/2 pkg. of alfalfa sprouts
Garlic sesame dressing

Mix all ingredients and serve.
*Submitted by NiMaatRa Niiquerty, Professor of Purification.

BABY ZUCCHINI SALAD

2 or more small zucchini per serving
Olive oil
Apple cider or balsamic vinegar

Cut small zucchini lengthwise into "pickles" but leave one end intact so they hold together. Steam lightly. Transfer to a bowl and drizzle with olive oil and vinegar. Cool to room temperature before serving.

ASPARAGUS GINGER SALAD

1 lb. asparagus, tough ends removed
6 cloves garlic, minced
1 inch ginger root grated, unpeeled
1/2 tsp. maple syrup
2 Tbs. tamari
2 tsp. sesame oil
1 Tbs. rice vinegar
1 1/2 tsp. cayenne pepper

Slice the asparagus into match sticks by cutting each stalk into 3" lengths, then slivering the lengths into thin strips with a sharp paring knife. Steam asparagus for 5 minutes or until crisp-tender. Toss warm asparagus with remaining ingredients and serve at room temperature. **Live Food Variation:** Do not steam asparagus, use raw, and marinate in sauce for one hour.

Serves 4

COUSCOUS SALAD

2 cups couscous
1/3 cup olive oil
3 Tbs. lemon juice
1/4 tsp. ground cumin
1/2 tsp. honey
1/3 cup pine nuts
1/4 cup fresh parsley, chopped
2 Tbs. fresh cilantro, chopped(optional)

Pour boiling water over the couscous. Let stand five minutes. Mix together olive oil, lemon juice, cumin and honey to make dressing. Lightly toast pine nuts in dry heavy skillet until golden. Fluff couscous with a fork. Add dressing, nuts and parsley; toss together. Top with fresh cilantro, if available. Serve at room temperature.

SPICY PASTA SALAD

2 cups cooked pasta
1/2 cup whole snow peas
1 red bell pepper
3 tsps sesame seeds
1/3 tsp. cayenne pepper
2 Tbs. sauce
3 Tbs. sesame oil
2 Tbs. lemon juice
4 tsps. minced garlic
4 tsps. minced onion

Mix all ingredients with drained, cooked pasta and let marinate 30 minutes before serving.

BEAN SPROUT & WATERCRESS SALAD

1 lb. mung bean sprouts, rinsed and dried
1 bunch watercress, rinsed, trimmed and dried
2 Tbs. balsamic vinegar
2 Tbs. natural soy sauce
1 Tbs. peanut oil
2 tsp. roasted sesame oil
1 clove garlic, pressed

Mix sprouts and watercress in a salad bowl. Whisk remaining ingredients together in a small bowl. Just before serving, pour dressing over salad and toss.

CARROT SALAD

Dressing:
4 1/2 Tbs. orange juice
3/4 tsp. cinnamon
2 1/2 Tbs. lemon juice
1 1/2 tsp. olive oil
3/4 tsp. kelp
3 Tbs. almond oil
1 1/2 tsp. maple syrup
Salad:
4 1/2 cups peeled carrots, grated
3/4 cup raw sunflower seeds (soak overnight)

Blend dressing ingredients together and set aside. Toss the salad ingredients. Toss salad with dressing. Garnish with fresh parsley sprigs.
Serves 6

EGGPLANT SALAD

2 medium eggplants (about 2 pounds)
2 tomatoes, coarsely chopped
1 small red onion, minced (1/2 cup)
1 clove garlic, minced
3 Tbs. lemon juice
2 tsp. olive oil
1 Tbs. minced parsley
1 tbs. minced fresh coriander
3/4 tsp. ground cumin
1/2 tsp. paprika
1/4 tsp. turmeric
Coriander leaves (garnish)

Trim the eggplants and cut in half lengthwise. Place on a cookie sheet, cut side down, and bake at 400 for 45 minutes, or until soft to the touch. (Or grill over hot coals until soft; exact time will depend on the heat of the coals.)

Remove from oven and set aside until cool enough to handle. Scrape the pulp from the skin; discard skin. Chop pulp coarsely. Place in a large bowl. Add the tomatoes, onion, garlic, lemon juice, oil, parsley, coriander,cumin, paprika and turmeric. Stir well to combine. Cover and chill. Garnish with coriander. **Live Food Variation:** Cube raw eggplant, add remaining ingredients, cover and chill.

Serves 6

TWO BEAN SALAD WITH FRESH HERBS

1/2 lb. string beans
2 1/2 cups cooked navy beans (about 1 cup raw)
1 medium Kirby cucumber, thinly sliced
1 small red bell pepper, finely diced
1/4 cup olive oil
Juice of 1/2 lemon, or more to taste
1/4 cup chopped fresh basil
1/4 cup chopped fresh parsley
1 tsp. maple syrup

Steam string beans until tender-crisp and rinse under cool water. Combine with remaining ingredients and toss gently. **Live Food Variation**: Use raw string beans, replace navy beans with raw green peas.

Serves 6

CAULIFLOWER/ARGUGULA SALAD

4 cups cauliflowerets
6 cups argula leaves
4 Tbs. extra-virgin olive oil
2 Tbs. balsamic vinegar
1 tsp. mustard
1 tsp. parsley flakes

Steam cauliflowerets crisp-tender, about 3 - 5 minutes; cool.

Line serving platter with arugula. Mound caulilflowerets in center.

In jar with tight-fitting lid, combine remaining ingredients, shake well to mix. Drizzle the dressing over; toss to coat well. **Live Food Variation:** Use finely chopped raw cauliflower.

Serves 6

MANGO STRAWBERRY SALAD

3 Tbs. agar-agar flakes
2 cups apple juice
3 Tbs. maple syrup
2 cups sliced strawberries
2 mangoes, sliced
1 Tbs. lemon juice

Add the agar-agar flakes to the apple juice in a saucepan. Bring to a boil, cover, reduce heat and simmer for 15 minutes to dissolve the agar-agar. Cool slightly. Add the maple syrup, strawberries, mangoes and lemon juice. Chill until set.

Serves 6

VEGETABLE SALAD

1/2 green leaf or red leaf lettuce
1/4 cup scallions, chopped
1/4 cup radish, chopped
1/2 cup cucumber, chopped
1/2 cup tomatoes, chopped
1/2 cup broccoli
1/2 cup cauliflower
1/2 cup alfalfa sprouts
1/2 cup olive oil
1/4 cup apple cider vinegar
1/8 tsp. fresh garlic
1/2 tsp. basil
1/4 tsp. paprika
Pinch of cayenne pepper

Combine all vegetables into a large bowl. Put remaining ingredients into a tight fitted jar and shake well. Pour over vegetables and toss lightly.

BLACKEYE PEA SALAD*

*2 cups cooked blackeyed peas
1 cup peeled tomatoes, chopped
1 cup carrots, shredded
1/2 cup yellow squash or zucchini, chopped
1 small onion, chopped
1/4 cup olive oil
1/4 tsp. basil
1/4 tsp. garlic, fresh
1 tsp. honey, if desired
Pinch of cayenne pepper*

Combine peas, tomatoes, carrots, squash, and onions in a large bowl. Put remaining ingredients into a tight fitted jar and shake well. Pour vegetable and toss to coat. Refrigerate salad for several hours until well chilled. **Live Food Variation:** Replace blackeyed peas with fresh cut green beans.

*Submitted by Dorothy Simons, Elder, Professor of Purification.

TOFU EGGLESS SALAD

1/2 cup mashed tofu
1/4 cup fine dried onions
1/4 tsp. tumeric
2 Tbs. oil
1/4 cup celery (add at the end)
1 tsp. yellow prepared mustard
1/4 tsp. granulated garlic
1/8 tsp. cayenne
1/2 cup soy mayonnaise (see recipe)

Saute the onions with oil and seasonings. Add the crushed tofu and continue to saute. Remove from heat and add the soy mayo and celery. Cool and serve as a sandwich on whole wheat bread or as a salad.

Serves 2

GUMBO SALAD

1 lb. okra
2 ears corn
Argula, or red leaf lettuce

Clean and cut okra. Cut corn kernels from cob. Mix okra and corn together, toss with a teriyaki sauce. Serve on a bed of argula or red leaf lettuce.

SPROUT SALAD

Combine any of the following sprouts:
Alfalfa
Clover
Radish
Bean
Sunflower

Serve on a bed of lettuce. Squeeze juice of fresh lemon
or use any dressing.

ROOT SALAD

2 carrots, grated
2 beets, grated
2 parsnips, grated

Combine all ingredients. Moisten with any sauce or
dressing. Serve on a bed of greens.

RELISH SALAD

1 green pepper, chopped in small pieces
1 red pepper, chopped in small pieces
2 ears of corn, kernels removed
1 small onion, finely chopped
Fresh herbs:
parsley, thyme or oregano, finely chopped

Combine all ingredients. Moisten with the dressing of choice.
Serve on a bed of salad greens.

MUSHROOM-SPINACH SALAD

1 3/4 cup spinach
1/2 cup sliced mushrooms
Dash of cayenne pepper
2 tsp. onion, chopped

Mix all ingredients. Moisten with dressing of choice.

Serves 4

A GOOD SALAD DOESN'T NEED ANY DRESSING! IDEALLY A
LITTLE FRESH LEMON JUICE WILL LIVEN UP AN ALREADY
LIVE MEAL. BUT, FOR THOSE WHO CANNOT RESIST ADDING
SALAD DRESSING, HERE ARE SOME HEALTHY YET TASTY
ALTERNATIVES

EGGLESS SOY MAYONNAISE

1 cup soy milk
4 tsp. honey
1-1 1/2 cups safflower oil
4 tsp. apple cider vinegar
1/8 tsp. cayenne pepper

Blend first 2 ingredients slowly adding oil. Put 2
ingredients in a bowl and whip in next 2 ingredients slowly.
As mixture stiffens add the last 2 ingredients. Mix well and
chill.

HERB VINEGAR

1/4 cup (packed) of fresh tarragon,
basil or dill, or 4 cloves peeled
garlic or ginger
2 cups vinegar

Heat vinegar to just below the boiling point. Add herbs
and place into jar; cover loosely with a towel. Let cool. When
cool, tightly cap and let sit at room temperature for one month.
Herbs may be left in or removed.

LEMON-GARLIC DRESSING

1 cup cider or wine vinegar
1 cup water
2 Tbs. lemon juice
1/2 cucumber, cut in chunks
1 small onion, cut in chunks
2 garlic cloves
1/4 tsp. cayenne pepper (optional)
1/2 tsp. celery seed
1/2 tsp. dill weed
1 Tbs. parsley flakes

Blend all ingredients until smooth. Refrigerate. Keeps well in refrigerator.
Makes 2 1/2 cups.

MISO DRESSING

3 Tbs. light miso
1 1/2 cup safflower oil
1/2 cup apple cider vinegar
1/2 cup tamari
1/2 cup water
1 - 2 tsps. grated fresh ginger root (unpeeled)
1/4 cup honey

Blend all ingredients until smooth.
Makes 2 cups.

SESAME GARLIC DRESSING

4 medium or large cloves of garlic minced
2 Tbs. basil
1 tsp. oregano
1/4 cup raw sesame seeds
1/2 cup water
1/2 cup of sesame oil
1 tsp. lemon juice
Sea salt & cayenne pepper to taste

Blend all ingredients, except oil, until smooth.
Slowly add oil. As oil blends in it will thicken
the dressing.

Soups & Stews

6

TRADITIONAL SOUP/STEWS RECIPES are "heavy." To help the digestive process, add flax seeds to the pot.

Those of you who are on the Natural Living program. Puree all soups/stews before consuming, adding water to thin as necessary. Soups with beans will be too glassy and should be avoided or eaten occasionally if you are on the program.

CREAM OF NAVY BEAN SOUP

1 lb. navy beans, soaked
3 quarts water
1 large yellow onion, chopped
4 stalks celery, with tops
2 tsp. curry powder
2 cups pureed tomatoes, blended
2 Tbs. safflower oil
Soy milk
Sprouts
Spinach leaves

In large dutch oven place beans, water, onion and celery. Cook for 1 1/2 hours. Add curry and tomato, cook until beans are tender, about 1 hour. Add oil and stir. Add milk to desired consistency. Reheat and serve.

VEGETABLE BROTH

2 cups carrots, thinly sliced
2 cups green pea pods
1 onion, sliced
6 celery tops
6 cups water
Outside leaves of lettuce, spinach or greens
Outside leaves of cabbage, shredded

Wash vegetables, slice and put into large saucepan. Cover with water. Bring to a boil and let simmer about 1/2 hour. Strain and serve.

SPLIT PEA SOUP

1/2 cup dry split peas
1/4 cup dry lima beans
1/8 cup rice
4 cups water
1 yellow onion, chopped
1 bay leaf
1/2 tsp. celery seed
1 carrot, sliced
1 stalk celery, sliced
1 potato, chopped
1/4 tsp. paprika
1 Tbs. parsley flakes (or
1/4 cup chopped fresh parsley)
1/2 tsp. basil
1/8 tsp. cayenne pepper

In a large pot, combine peas, lima beans, rice, water, onion, bay leaf and celery seed, Bring to a boil, reduce heat, cover and simmer for 1 1/2 hours. Add remaining ingredients, cover and simmer an additional 45 minutes. Remove bay leaf before serving.

Serves 4

CARROT SOUP

3 large carrots, chopped
1 small onion, chopped
1 potato, peeled and chopped
4 cups water
1/4 tsp. ground ginger
1/8 tsp. ground nutmeg
1 tsp. lemon juice

Combine all ingredients in a saucepan. Bring to a boil, reduce heat, cover and simmer for 15 minutes. In a blender or food processor, blend soup until smooth. Return to pan and heat through. Garnish with chopped fresh parsley or coriander.

Serves 4

ZUCCHINI SOUP

1 onion
4 cups water
4 large zucchini, cut in chunks
1/3 cup fresh dill, finely chopped
2 Tbs. soy sauce
Dash of garlic powder

Cook the onion in 1/2 cup of water in a medium saucepan for five minutes. Add the remaining water, and the rest of the ingredients. Bring to a boil, reduce heat, cover and simmer about 20 minutes. Process in blender, small amounts at a time, until velvety smooth. Serve warm.

Serves 6

SEAWEED VEGETABLE SOUP

4 tsp. water, for sauteing
2 small strips kombu
1 yellow onion, sliced into thin strips
1 large carrot, sliced
1 cup orange squash (acorn or hubbard is good)
peeled and cut into small cubes
1 cup broccoli florets
3 cups water seasoned with tamari, pepper
or nutritional yeast
2 tsp. basil
1/2 tsp. marjoram
1/2 tsp. soy sauce
Freshly minced parsley for garnish

Heat water in soup pot and add kombu (keep in strips). Stir in onion. Saute over medium high heat until onion is soft but not browned. Add carrot, squash and broccoli. Cook for two minutes. Add seasoned water, basil and marjoram and bring to a boil. Lower heat to medium and cook, covered, for 20 minutes or until squash is soft. Season with tamari and garnish with parsley. Before serving, slice kombu into thin strips and serve in soup.

Serves 4 - 6

VEGETABLE STEW

1 lb. lentils
5 cups water or vegetable broth
6 Tbs. water for sauteing
2 leeks, thinly sliced
1 clove garlic, mashed
4 carrots, thinly sliced
2 stalks celery, thinly sliced
4 large potatoes, cubed
2 small white turnips, cubed
2 cups tomatoes, peeled and drained
(fresh or canned)
1/2 tsp. cayenne pepper
1 tsp. Fines herbs
2 Tbs. fresh parsley, chopped

Cook lentils by bringing to a boil, cover and simmer about 45 minutes. Saute leeks in water about five minutes. Add garlic, carrots, celery, potatoes and turnips. Cook 10 minutes more, stirring, over low heat. Add cooked vegetables to lentils. Add tomatoes, pepper and herbs. Simmer 20 minutes, uncovered, or until vegetables are tender. Mash some of the lentils with a potato masher if thickening is not needed. Serve hot, sprinkle with parsley

POTATO LEEK SOUP

3 Tbs. soy margarine
1 cup minced onion
3 cups sliced potatoes
1 cup sliced celery
1 cup sliced leeks
2 cups thinly sliced carrots
4 cups water
1 tsp. maple syrup

Melt margarine in a large skillet. Add the potatoes and onion, and saute gently for about five minutes, stirring to prevent sticking. Add the leeks, half the carrots and celery and the water. Bring to a boil, then reduce heat and simmer gently for about 20 minutes, stirring occasionally. Meanwhile, steam the remaining carrots until tender.

When the potato-leek mixture is cooked, puree it in a blender. If the puree is too thick, add water to thin it, then add the maple syrup. Reheat before serving. Float some of the steamed carrot slices on each serving.

Serves 4

Marinade/Sauces Dips

7

*T*HE GREAT THING ABOUT MARINADE, sauce or dip is that they add a zip to any veggie, pasta or tofu dish. Use on raw, steamed grilled or sauted vegetables, tofu or tempeh

SESAME SAUCE

3 Tbs. sesame paste
4 Tbs. soy sauce
1 Tbs. sesame oil

In a bowl slowly add soy sauce to tahini and blend well. Stir in sesame oil.

HOISIN SAUCE

1/4 cup miso
2 tsp. toasted sesame oil
1/4 cup honey
1 tsp. soy sauce
2 Tbs. water
1 1/2 tsp. apple cider vinegar

Combine all ingredients and mix well.

GINGERY TAHINI SAUCE

1/2 cup tahini sauce
1 Tbs. mustard
1 Tbs. miso
1 tsp. ginger juice
1 Tbs. rice or umeboshi vinegar
1 1/1 - 2 cups water

Puree all ingredients in blender until smooth.   In a saucepan, heat slowly over a low flame, do not boil! Add water to obtain desired consistency. Tastes great over noodles.

CREAMY TOFU DIP
WITH GARLIC & DILL

8 oz. soft tofu
3 Tbs. lemon juice
2 Tbs. safflower oil
1 Tbs. tamari (or to taste)
3 large cloves garlic
1 1/2 tsp. dill weed
1 1/2 tsp. parsley, finely minced

In a blender, blend lemon juice and garlic until garlic is minced very fine. Add remaining ingredients except parsley and puree until smooth. Stir in parsley.

MUSTARD MARINADE

2 Tbs. dijon-style mustard
3 cloves garlic, crushed
3 Tbs. tamari or soy sauce
3 Tbs. lemon or lime juice
1 Tbs. vegetable oil

Mix all ingredients except oil. Add the oil 1/2 teaspoon at a time, mixing vigorously after each addition.
Makes 5 ounces

SWEET AND TANGY MARINADE

3 Tbs. vegetable oil
1/2 cup cider vinegar
3/4 cup ketchup
1/4 cup soy sauce
1 Tbs. molasses
3 Tbs. maple syrup
Pinch allspice

Bring all ingredients to a boil, cover, reduce heat and simmer 5 minutes. Cool.
Makes 2 cups

APPLE GINGER MARINADE

1/4 cup apple juice or cider
1 Tbs. minced fresh ginger
1/4 cup cider vinegar
1/3 cup vegetable oil
1/3 cup tamari
1/3 cup honey
2 cloves garlic, crushed

Mix all ingredients.

HOMEMADE TERIYAKI SAUCE

1/2 cup tamari or soy sauce
1/4 cup rice vinegar
1 Tbs. sake, mirin or white wine (optional)
1 Tbs. rice syrup or honey
Dash hot pepper sauce
1 tsp. toasted sesame oil

Whisk together ingredients.
Makes 1 cup.

MUSTARD

1/4 cup ground brown mustard seeds
3 Tbs. boiling water
1 Tbs. olive oil
1/4 tsp. maple syrup

Mix all ingredients together.

TOFU "SOUR CREAM"

1/2 lb. tofu
2 - 3 Tbs. lemon juice
1/4 herbal seasoning
3 Tbs. oil
Water

Blend all ingredients, except oil, until creamy. Gradually add oil while still blending. For tartness add more lemon juice. If too thick, add a little water.

Makes 1 cup

SPIRULINA SAUCE

4 Tbs. water for sauteing
1 onion, chopped
2 cloves garlic, minced
4 cups assorted fresh vegetables, chopped
2 Tbs. whole wheat flour
1 Tbs. spirulina

Saute onion and garlic in water for 5 minutes, or until soft. Slightly steam vegetables. Dilute the flour in the water. Simmer until thickened. Stir in spirulina. Pour sauce over steamed vegetables.

TOFU COTTAGE CHEESE

1 cup mashed tofu
1/2 cup onion, chopped fine
3 tsp. water for sauteing
1/4 tsp. dillweed
1/2 cup soy mayonnaise (see recipe)
2 Tbs. chopped chives

Saute the onions in the water with the seasonings. Cool. Add the mashed tofu, chives and soy mayo. Cool and serve as a salad.

Makes 2 cups

SOY MAYONNAISE

1 1/2 lbs. tofu
3/4 cups oil
2 Tbs. apple cider vinegar
1 cup water
1 Tbs. mustard
1/4 tsp. granulated garlic
1/8 medium onion
1/2 tsp. cayenne pepper (optional)
2 Tbs. lemon juice
1 Tbs. cashew meal (optional if using a firmer tofu)

Blend all ingredients until smooth.

Main Dishes

8

ONE OF THE MANY THINGS I HAVE LEARNED over the
years is, that as a vegetarian, I didn't have to give up all of the
foods I grew up on. Many recipes could be adapted without the
meat, and there are alternatives for salt, sugar and oil.

One of my favorite stories, is of a Super Bowl party that
I would have every year with lots of food. Being the only
vegetarian, the regulars were used to eating a vegetarian meal.
I always gave them the option of bringing a meat dish if the had
to have meat, (no one ever did!). One year I decided to make
chili. I used tofu that had been frozen, thawed and crumbled to
give a ground beef texture. As the hostess, I was the last to begin
eating. As I did a few of my guests stopped and looked at me in
disbelief. I knew immediately what was on their minds. I
smiled and said, "that's tofu, not ground beef you're eating".
Everyone was amazed that they could not tell the difference!

A word of caution, many of our favorite meals even with
the adaptions are still too "heavy" for a natural living diet.
Always limit how often you eat grains, nuts and beans. Many

of the following recipes call for serving over rice or noodles. As you progress on your natural living diet, fix the recipe but omit the grain or noodle and use the live food variation.

If you are in transition from a meat based diet to a vegetarian diet or cook for meat eaters, these recipes will be a refreshing change.

"VEGETABLE DISHES"

CURRY MIXED VEGETABLES

2 cups cooked brown rice
1 cup string beans cut in thirds
2 cups shredded cabbage
1 onion, chopped
4 cloves of garlic
1 cup mushrooms, sliced
1 cup ginger tea (1 tsp. ginger, 1/2 orange peel)
1 large green pepper
3 Tbs. curry (to taste)
1 Tbs. soy sauce
Pinch of cayenne (to taste)

Heat pan. Put garlic, onion, green pepper, mushrooms and tea (enough to cover vegetables) in pan. Simmer until mushrooms are tender. Add soy sauce and curry. Stir well. Add remaining vegetables and tea. Steam until vegetables turn bright green, approximately 5 minutes. Add rice. Stir well.

STUFFED SQUASH

2 medium acorn squash
2 medium carrots, chopped
2 Tbs. maple syrup
1 tsp. cinnamon and nutmeg

Cut squash in 1/2 and clean out seeds. Place cut side down in baking dish. Cover. Bake at 350 degrees for 30 minutes. Turn cut side up, bake for 30 minutes longer. Scoop pulp out of each half, keeping shells intact. Place cooked pulp in bowl and set aside. Meanwhile, steam carrots until tender. Add to cooked squash pulp. Mix together until mashed. Stir in maple syrup, cinnamon and nutmeg. Spoon into reserved squash shells. Bake, uncovered, at 350 degrees for 15 minutes.

Serves 8

DANDELION GREENS*

2 lbs. dandelion greens
2 Tbs. olive oil
1/2 tsp. cayenne
ginger
tahini (sesame)
Herbs
2 Tbs. water

Remove roots and pick over carefully, washing in several waters. Dry between paper towels. Heat water, stir in greens, cover wok or skillet tightly; steam for 10 minutes over low heat. Add olive oil, chop, season accordingly and serve. **Note:** Top with sesame tahini.

Serves 4

*Submitted by Rabiah Latif, Professor of Purification.

TURNIP GREENS

2 lbs. turnip greens
2 cups water
2 Tbs. safflower oil
2 cubes vegetable bouillon
1 clove garlic, chopped
1 large red onion, chopped
1 tsp. soy sauce
1/2 tsp. basil
1 bay leaf
1/8 tsp. dill
1/4 tsp. oregano
1 Tbs. soy margarine

Wash greens and cut into tiny pieces. Bring water to a boil in saucepan; add bouillon cubes. Simmer until the cubes dissolve. Place greens in a large skillet or wok. Cover with seasoned water. Add remaining ingredients. Cover and simmer until tender 10 - 15 minutes. Add oil after greens have cooked and remove bay leaf.

Serves 4

KALE (STEAMED)

Boiling water
fresh kale
1/2 tsp. cayenne
lemon juice
1/2 tsp. caraway seeds or ground ginger
tahini (sesame)

After removing roots and cleaning thoroughly, dry between paper towels. Chill until ready to use. Tear into shreds if leaves are large. Drop into a little water along with seasonings, cover and steam 5 - 6 minutes. Add lemon juice top with sesame tahini and serve.

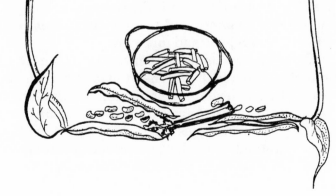

TOFU CREOLE

2/3 cup vegetable oil: 1/2 cup flour
1 3/4 cup shallots (scallions), thinly sliced
1/3 cup chopped celery
1 cup chopped onion
1/2 cup chopped green pepper
4 tsp. garlic, finely minced
1 - 1 lb. Italian style whole peeled tomatoes
1 - 8 oz. jar tomato sauce : 1 tbs. minced chives
4 whole bay leaves, crushed
6 whole allspice : 2 whole cloves
1/2 tsp. cayenne : 1/4 tsp. chili powder
1/4 tsp. mace : 1/4 tsp. dried basil
1/2 tsp. dried thyme : 4 tsp. fresh lemon juice
2 cups water : 2 lb. cubed tofu, thawed

In a heavy 6 - 8 quart pot or kettle, heat oil and gradually add flour, stirring constantly. Cook over low heat, stirring constantly, until a medium brown roux (the color of rich peanut butter) if formed. Remove from the heat, add fresh vegetables and parsley. Mix well with the roux, then return to low heat and cook, stirring constantly, until the vegetables begin to brown. Mix in canned tomatoes and tomato sauce, then add chives, seasonings, lemon juice and mix again.

Raise the heat under the pan and bring to a low boil. Add water and mix thoroughly. When the mixture boils up again, reduce the heat and simmer for 45 minutes. Add the tofu and allow to come to a low boil again, then cover, reduce heat slightly and simmer for 20 minutes. Remove the pot from the burner and allow to stand covered, at room temperature for about 10 minutes before serving. Serve over brown rice.

RATATOUILLE

3 cups eggplant, cubed
2 cups zucchini, sliced
1 green pepper, chopped
1 clove garlic, minced
1/4 cup olive oil
1/4 cup water
2 Tbs. fresh chopped parsley
2 tomatoes, chopped

Combine all ingredients except the parsley, oil and tomatoes in a skillet and cook covered over medium heat 10 - 15 minutes until the vegetables are tender. Add the parsley and tomatoes. Cook another 5 minutes. Remove from heat, add oil and stir well. Serve hot or cold. **Live Food Variation:** Do not cook vegetables, mix all ingredients and marinate for at least 2 hours.

Serves 6

SAVORY DAIKON

4 - 6 1/2 Tbs. water
4 cups daikon or turnip, coarsely shredded
(loosely packed)
1 Tbs. soy sauce
Large pinch date sugar or drop of maple syrup
2 tsp. green onion, minced

Heat water over a high flame. When water is hot, add daikon or turnip, lower heat to medium-high or medium, stir-fry 3 1/2 minutes. While cooking, mash vegetable frequently and firmly to ensure even, complete cooking. Remove from heat and sprinkle with soy sauce, date sugar, and onion. Mix and mash another minute or so. Serve warm.

Serves 3 - 4

MARINATED BROCCOLI & CAULIFLOWER

1/2 lb. fresh broccoli
1/2 head of cauliflower
1/4 cup apple cider vinegar
2 tsp. lemon juice
1 tsp. basil
1 tsp. dill

Wash vegetables and cut them into flowers. In a bowl combine ingredients add vegetables and marinate 5 - 7 hours in a covered glass dish in the refrigerator. Serve at room temperature.

SEAWEED GUMBO

2 lbs. okra
1/2 pkg. hiziki seaweed
1/2 pkg. mekabu or wakame seaweed
2 bay leaves
1/2 cup chopped parsley
4 cups boiling water
2 green peppers, chopped
5 ripe tomatoes
1 pkg. black mushrooms
1 pkg. oyster mushrooms
l large chopped onion
1/4 tsp. thyme
1/4 cup water
2 cups chopped celery
Cayenne pepper (to taste)

Saute onions, pepper, celery in water. Chop and saute okra; cook until okra is bright green. Puree tomatoes and add to onions, celery and peppers. Soak seaweed in water, then cut in bite-sized pieces. Simmer tomato mixture for 15 minutes, then add boiling water. Add mushrooms, seaweed, cayenne, thyme and parsley. Cook at a low simmer for 3 - 4 hours, adding okra 1/2 hour before serving. Serve over rice.

TOFU STUFFED PEPPERS

5 oz. water
1 onion, chopped
1 garlic clove, chopped
14 oz. tofu, squeezed and mashed or
2 oz. wild rice, cooked
1 tsp. oregano
1/2 tsp. basil
4 red peppers, medium cayenne pepper

Heat water and saute the onions and garlic until transparent.

Add the crumbled tofu or wild rice, oregano and basil.

Cook ingredients for 5 minutes, stirring constantly to avoid burning the onions.

Add cayenne pepper, set aside to cool slightly.

Cut off the bottoms of the peppers, remove seeds and wash the peppers.

Fill the peppers with the tofu mixture and steam them for 10 - 15 minutes or until the stuffing is heated through.

Live Food Variation: Replace wild rice or tofu with finely chopped cauliflower and grated carrots. Combine all ingredients—do not saute garlic or onions—and stuff peppers.

SESAME STRING BEANS

1 lb. string beans
1 clove garlic, crushed
1/2 cup water
4 Tbs. sesame oil
3 Tbs. apple cider vinegar
1/2 tsp. cayenne pepper
1/2 cup toasted sesame seeds

Steam beans until bright green and somewhat crisp. Douse in ice water and let them sit until chilled, changing water if necessary.

In a small skillet, saute the garlic in water. Add sesame oil, vinegar and pepper. Heat gently for several minutes until mixture is hot. Meanwhile, toast sesame seeds in a cast iron skillet until brown. No oil is needed, but watch the seeds carefully, since they tend to burn easily.

Drain beans and pat dry. Toss with hot oil mixture and sesame seeds. Serve immediately. **Live Food Variation:** Use raw string beans. Combine remaining ingredients—without heating—and marinate for at least 1 hour.

Serves 4

GRILLED CORN ON THE COB

1/3 cup soy margarine, softened
1 1/2 Tbs. minced fresh parsley leaves
1 1/2 Tbs. snipped fresh chives
1 1/2 Tbs. fresh thyme
1 1/2 Tbs. minced scallion
1 tsp. fresh lemon juice
8 ears of fresh corn
Hot sauce to taste

Combine all ingredients except corn in a bowl. Let stand at least 1 hour or overnight. Let mixture soften to a spreadable consistency. Peel back but do not remove the husks from the corn and discard the silk. Spread each ear with two teaspoons of the herb butter, wrap the husks carefully around the corn and wrap each ear in foil.

Roast the corn on a grill over hot coals, turning occasionally, for about 20 minutes or until the kernels are tender. Unwrap the corn, remove the husks and serve hot.

CAULIFLOWER PILAF

1 head of cauliflower
1 scallion, finely chopped
1 ear of corn, raw, kernels removed
1 red pepper, finely chopped
1 green pepper, finely chopped
Fresh herbs, to taste

In a food processor, chop cauliflower until its the consistency of a grain. Mix all ingredients. Add dressing or sauce to moisten. Serve on a bed of lettuce or grated carrots.

AVOCADO SUPREME

2 - 3 ripe avocadoes, sliced
1 tomato, cut in wedges
1 bunch of scallions, finely chopped
1 small garlic, minced
1 lemon, juiced
1/8 tsp. kelp

Mix all ingredients and serve on a bed of fresh greens.

"GRAINED BASED DISHES"

RICE MUSHROOM CASSEROLE

1 cup brown rice
2 onions, chopped
1/2 lb. mushrooms, chopped
2 cups boiling water
1/2 tsp. thyme
1/4 tsp. garlic powder
1/2 Tbs. soy sauce
2 Tbs. wheat germ

Saute onions in one-quarter cup for 10 minutes. Add mushrooms to pot and cook five minutes longer. Add rice, cook and stir for five minutes longer. Remove from heat. Add two cups boiling water, seasonings and wheat germ. Mix well. Pour into a casserole dish, cover, and bake in a 350 degree oven for 1 1/4 hours. Serve plain or with a sauce. This dish may be prepared ahead; add 30 minutes to baking time.

Serves 6

VEGETARIAN PAELLA

1 cup uncooked brown basmati rice
2 cups boiling water
3 tsp. water
1/2 cup chopped onion
3 cloves garlic, minced
1/2 cup each: sliced green bell pepper
and sliced red bell pepper
1/2 cup diced tomato
2 small red potatoes, thinly sliced
2 cups hot water flavored with soy sauce
and fresh herbs
1 tsp. saffron
3/4 tsp. oregano
5 marinated artichoke hearts
1 cup peas (fresh or frozen)*

Let rice stand for 20 minutes in water, then drain.

In a large, heavy skillet, heat water and saute onion and garlic until onion is soft. Add bell peppers, tomato and potatoes. Saute vegetables, about 3 minutes. Add rice and flavored water. Bring to a boil, then lower heat to simmer. Add saffron and oregano. Cover pot and let simmer until rice is tender (about 35 minutes for brown basmati).

Arrange artichokes and peas on top of rice,(* if you cannot find fresh peas, buy frozen peas with no salt added. There are organic frozen peas in your local health food store.), cover and cook until peas turn bright green, about 1 minute. Serve hot.

Serves 8

VEGETABLE PULAO RICE

2 1/2 cups basmati rice
1/4 cup water
1 medium onion, diced
6 - 8 cloves
2 bay leaves
6 - 8 black peppercorns
1 tsp. cumin seeds
1 two-inch long cinnamon stick
1/2 tsp. finely ground chili powder
1/2 cup green peas
1/2 cup diced carrots
2 1/2 pints of water

Wash the rice and drain. Put water in a saucepan over medium heat. When the water gets hot, add cloves, black peppercorns, cumin seeds, cinnamon stick, bay leaves and stir for a minute. Add onions, carrots, peas and chili powder. Stir for another 5 minutes. Reduce heat and add rice followed by water. Bring it to a boil and reduce to medium heat until the water is absorbed. Then cover and let cook on simmer for 20 minutes until the rice gets tender, soft and fluffy.

"NOODLE BASED DISHES"

SWEET 'N SOUR NOODLES

1 pkg. clear noodles, somen or udon
3 tsp. water for sauteing
2 slices ginger root, peeled
1 medium onion, thinly sliced
2 ribs celery, thinly sliced
2 medium carrots, thinly sliced
1 small red or green bell pepper,
seeded and sliced
2 cups bite-sized broccoli florets and stalks
1/2 to 2/3 cup water
1/4 cup rice vinegar
3 Tbs. maple syrup
1 Tbs. soy sauce
1 to 1 1/2 Tbs. arrowroot dissolved
in an equal amount of water

Cook noodles according to package directions and rinse until cool. Saute ginger, celery, onion, carrot and bell pepper in hot water for 2 - 3 minutes. Cover and cook 5 minutes. Add broccoli, cover an cook about 5 minutes more (until broccoli is just tender but still bright green). Uncover pan, remove from heat, and discard the ginger.

In small saucepan, combine water, vinegar, maple syrup and soy sauce. Bring the mixture to a gentle simmer, then remove from heat. Slowly pour in dissolved arrowroot stirring briskly. Return pan to heat and simmer for 1 - 2 minutes, stirring constantly. Mix the sauce with the vegetables and serve over the noodles. **Variation: Add 1 pound tofu cubed, adding tofu when broccoli is added. Serve without noodles.** **Serves 2**

NOODLES WITH
SESAME-GINGER SAUCE

1 pkg. udon, somen or soba (or any pasta)
1/4 cup water
1/4 cup tahini
1 1/2 tsp. soy sauce
1 Tbs. lemon juice
1 Tbs. mirin (optional)
1/4 cup water
1 Tbs. lemon juice
1 Tbs. juice of grated ginger root
1 small clove garlic, finely minced

Cook noodles according to package directions, rinse until cool. In a medium sized saucepan, add 1/4 cup water to tahini a little at a time, mixing well to form a smooth sauce. Add all remaining ingredients; bring to a simmer over medium heat. Gently simmer 1 minute. (The sauce will thicken as it cooks. If it becomes too thick, add a little water.) Ladle sauce over noodles in individual serving

PASTA AND BROCCOLI

12 oz. whole wheat pasta
Water for boiling
1 lb. broccoli, cut
2 large cloves garlic, minced
1/4 - 1/2 tsp. cayenne
3 1/2 cups diced fresh tomatoes

Cook pasta in boiling water until tender. Steam broccoli until tender-crisp, about 3 minutes. Set aside.

In a large skillet saute garlic and cayenne in water for 1 minute. Add tomatoes and cook over medium heat for 5 -10 minutes. Add broccoli. Serve over cooked pasta.

Serves 6-8

BAKED MACARONI AND CHEESE

1 cup nutritional yeast
1/3 cup whole wheat flour
2 cups water
1 large onion
1/2 cup soy margarine
2 tsp. mustard
3 1/2 cups cooked elbow macaroni
Pinch of paprika

Mix the dry ingredients together in a saucepan. Gradually add the water making a smooth paste by beating the mixture with a whisk. Continue to add water until the paste is thinned out. Place on a medium to low heat and stir constantly with a whisk until it thickens and bubbles. Let it bubble for 30 seconds and remove from heat. Whip in the margarine and mustard and grated onion. Mix half of the sauce with the drained macaroni and put in casserole dish. Put remaining macaroni and sauce on top. Sprinkle with paprika and bake for 15 minutes in a 350 degree preheated oven. Put in broiler for a few minutes until "cheese" sauce is stretchy and crisp.

Serves 6 - 8

*THIS IS A VERY "HEAVY" DISH. IT SHOULD BE PREPARED ON RARE OCCASIONS. NEXT TIME YOU'RE HAVING YOUR FAMILY THAT CAN NOT EAT WITHOUT AT LEAST ONE OF THE "TRADITIONAL" DISHES, SERVE THIS.

TO HELP DIGEST HEAVY STARCH MEALS, DRINK JUICE OF ONE LEMON WITH WARM WATER 1/2 HOUR PRIOR TO MEAL.

TOFU MEXICAN STYLE

1 onion, chopped fine
1 green bell pepper, chopped medium
1 red bell pepper, chopped medium
1 lb. firm tofu, crumbled (be sure to squeeze out
excess water)
1/2 tsp. oregano
1/2 tsp. chili powder
1/2 tsp. cumin powder
1/4 tsp. black pepper, finely ground
1/2 tsp. tumeric powder
1/8 tsp. cayenne pepper, finely ground
2 cups whole tomatoes, blanched, seeded and diced
6 Tbs. water

Steam the vegetables for several minutes. In a separate pan, simmer tomatoes and tofu with seasonings. Add steamed vegetables and serve.

Serves 4

TOFU WITH GINGER AND ONION

16 oz. regular or firm tofu
2 tsp. ginger root, minced
1 Tbs. green onion, minced, or
3 Tbs. soy sauce
2 tsp. sesame oil

Cut the tofu into one-inch cubes and place in a bowl. Toss gently, using chopsticks, with the remaining ingredients. Toss two or three times at intervals until the dressing is absorbed. This should take only a few minutes at most.

TIP: To remove excess water from tofu, drain tofu and press between two plates (add weight to top plate if necessary.)

TOFU LOAF

28 oz. firm tofu, drained and mashed
1 2/3 cups rolled oats
3/4 cup whole wheat bread crumbs
1/3 cup ketchup
5 Tbs. soy sauce
2 Tbs. dijon mustard
1/4 tsp. garlic powder (optional)
1/4 tsp. cayenne pepper (optional)

Combine all ingredients in a large bowl. Mix well. Press mixture into a lightly oiled loaf pan. Bake at 350 degrees for 1 hour. Let cool for 15 minutes, then remove from pan.

CURRIED TOFU

1 onion, chopped
2 cloves garlic, minced
5 Tbs. water
1 tsp. curry powder
1 lb. tofu, drained and cubed
1 cup peas
1 carrot, diced
1 celery, diced

Saute onion and garlic in water. Add remaining ingredients and cook over medium heat for 10 - 20 minutes, adding extra water if needed to prevent sticking. Serve.

Serves 4

TEMPEH JAMBALAYA

1/2 lb. tempeh, cut into 1/2 inch squares
1 large onion, chopped
2 - 5 cloves garlic, minced
2 carrots, diced, about 1 cup
1 green pepper, diced
2 stalks celery, chopped
2 tsp. water
2 bay leaves
1 cup long grain brown rice
2 cups water
Pinch each of the following seasonings:
cayenne, oregano, chili powder
cloves, nutmeg or mace
Chopped parsley or scallions for garnish

Cut tempeh into squares. In a skillet, saute tempeh in water about 3 minutes. Set aside. In a heavy pot with a tight-fitting lid heat the 2 tsp. water. Add the vegetables; saute for a few minutes. Add tempeh, spices and rice; stir to coat. Next, add water and stir again, Cover, bring mixture to a boil, lower heat, simmer (or pressure cook) for 45 minutes, until liquid is absorbed. Fluff with a fork and garnish with parsley or scallions.

Serves 4 - 6

TOFU &
CHERRY TOMATO KEBOBS

1 bottle natural barbecue sauce
1 Tbs. miso
1 1/2 cakes tofu, cut into cubes slightly
smaller than the cherry tomatoes
1 pint cherry tomatoes

In a medium bowl, combine the barbecue sauce and miso.
Add the tofu cubes and marinate for at least and hour,
turning occasionally.
To grill, alternate the tofu cubes and cherry tomatoes on
greased bamboo or metal skewers. Grill over hot coals for 10 -
15 minutes, turning occasionally.

Serves 4 - 6

Children's Menus

9

AN Y PARENT OF A SMALL CHILD will tell you their child either does not like meat or will eat very little meat. It is only with continual feeding of adult preferences that children develop such tastes. Remember processed baby foods used to be made with salt and sugar for the mother's taste buds, not the child's. If we enhance our child's natural instinct and guide them in developing sound healthy eating habits, we have given them the greatest gift!

The concern most parents have is what about my children. Will they eat a vegetarian diet? Will they eat all they need? Will they succumb to peer pressure?

Children adapt easily. If they are raised from birth as vegetarians, with a healthy outlook they will flourish and grow.

If the family is making the transition to vegetarianism, be mindful that if it's hard on you sometimes, it will be the same for your children.

The key is to communicate with your child the reasons why you've chosen this lifestyle. Remember the growing process is to challenge and experiment. By being flexible and creative your child can still experiment within acceptable limits.

Golden Rule: IF YOU DON'T WANT YOUR CHILD EATING CERTAIN FOODS YOU <u>MUST NOT</u> EAT THOSE FOODS OR HAVE THEM IN YOUR HOME.

One day Kali-my 3 1/2 year old from birth vegan-came home from school and told me she did not want to be a vegetarian anymore. When I asked why she said because gum had sugar in it and she wanted to chew gum. I told her she could still be a vegetarian and chew gum that didn't have sugar in it. We went to the health food store and purchased sugarless chewing gum (of course I was cringing inside during this whole episode). Kali chewed it and told me it tasted bad. The subject has never come up again.

The following recipes are suitable for lunches.

"SANDWICHES"

POCKET FILLERS

Whole wheat pita pockets are excellent to pack in a child's or adult's lunch.

Any of the following spreads can be used. Add sprouts, cucumbers, lettuce or tomatoes.

REMEMBER: As you make progress on your diet, breads should be eaten sparingly and eventually omitted. All of these sandwiches can be eaten without bread. Use on greens or eat alone. Fillings can be carried in a tight fitting container.

VEGGIE POCKET

Grated carrots, and/or beets with sprouts, lettuce and cucumbers. Add raw or roasted sesame seeds. **Variations:** The veggie pocket can be made without the pita bread.

"SPREADS & FILLINGS"

SESAME SPREAD

1/3 cup sesame butter
2 Tbs. chopped sunflower seeds

Mix together all ingredients and spread on toasted whole wheat bread. **Variation:** Spread on a large rice cake or serve on a bed of lettuce.

TOFU SPREAD

1/2 lb. tofu
1/2 tsp. grated lemon peel
1 - 2 Tbs. lemon juice
1 - 2 Tbs. honey

Combine and mash all ingredients well with a fork, or puree in a food processor. Serve on a bed of salad greens with grated carrots or beets.

Makes 1 1/2 cups

GUACAMOLE

2 medium avocadoes, peeled and mashed
1 tomato, finely chopped
(peel for a smoother consistency)
1 Tbs. minced onion
1 Tbs. chopped fresh cilantro or parsley
1 Tbs. fresh lemon juice

Combine all ingredients in a wooden or ceramic bowl (do not use metal or it will cause discoloration in the avocado). Mix well. Serve on a bed of lettuce with grated carrots or beets.

HUMUS

1 1/2 cups raw chickpeas, cooked and cooled
2 large cloves garlic
2 tsp. tamari
Juice from 2 medium lemons
1/2 - 3/4 cup tahini (sesame butter)
1/8 cup minced parsley
3 Tbs. red onion, finely minced

Use as a spread on rice cakes or to fill a pita pocket.

NOTE: Nori sheets, sushi, can make an excellent substitute for sandwich bread

SUSHI ROLL-UPS

2 cups cooked short-grain brown rice
4 sheets nori, lightly toasted
1 green onion, sliced lengthwise into 4 strips
1 red bell pepper, sliced into 16 thin strips
8 leaves fresh spinach
1/4 cup sesame seeds, lightly toasted,
(reserve 1/8 tsp. for garnish)

Place one sheet of nori on a clean dishtowel or sushi mat, and spoon 1/2 cup rice on top. Spread rice evenly to edges of nori. Line a strip onion, four strips of bell pepper and two spinach leaves in center. Sprinkle with sesame seeds. Roll into a tight roll and press to seal edges. Slice into pieces.

Variations: Use mashed tofu, shredded carrots, beets and mashed avocado to replace brown rice. Better yet, use the pulp from your juicer as a filler.

Desserts

10

Oh! Do I have to give up all my gooey, sugary desserts?

For a healthier lifestyle, yes you do! However, I think the following recipes will be a healthy alternative while you make the transition. They will spur you on to create your own healthy alternatives and have some fun doing so.

But, remember, desserts no matter how healthy should be eaten occasionally.

COOKIES
TAHINI COOKIES

Dry Ingredients:
3 cups whole wheat pastry flour
Liquid Ingredients:
1 lb. tahini sauce
2/3 cup liquid lecithin
3/4 cup maple syrup
1 tsp. vanilla extract

Sift flour into a mixing bowl. In a separate bowl, cream tahini sauce, maple syrup and vanilla together until smooth. Add flour to tahini mixture and stir to mix evenly. Preheat oven to 350 degrees. Lightly oil cookie sheet. Form dough into walnut sized balls, and press with a fork. Bake 10 - 15 minutes, until light brown. Cookies will be crumbly while hot. Allow to cool 10 minutes, then remove from tray.

Makes 30 small cookies.

GINGER COOKIES

1/2 cup molasses
1 Tbs. liquid lecithin
1/2 tsp. baking soda
1 tsp. hot water
1 1/2 tsp. ground ginger
1/2 tsp. cinnamon
1 3/4 cups whole wheat flour

Combine molasses, lecithin, baking soda dissolved in hot water, ginger and cinnamon. Add enough flour to make a dough firm enough to roll; use your hands if necessary. Roll thinly on a floured surface and cut into shapes with a cookie cutter. Place on a greased baking sheet and bake at 350 degrees for about 10 minutes. Transfer to a wire rack to cool.

Makes 2 dozen cookies.

ALMOND COOKIES

3/4 cup almonds
2 Tbs. liquid lecithin
1/4 cup real maple syrup
3/4 tsp. vanilla
1/4 tsp. almond extract
1/4 tsp. cinnamon
2/3 cup rolled oats
2 Tbs. water

Preheat oven to 350 degrees Use a food processor or a blender to make the cookie batter. First, process the almonds until coarsely chopped.   Add remaining ingredients except water and pulse briefly to mix. Turn machine on and add 1 1/2 - 2 tablespoons water, or just enough to moisten. Scrape down the sides of the machine and mix again.

Use a spoon to pat out 10 cookie rounds onto a greased baking sheet.   Bake about 25 minutes, until light brown. Remove immediately from pan using a metal spatula.

"CAKES & FROSTINGS"

NO-BAKE BLUEBERRY COUSCOUS CAKE*

5 cups apple or apricot juice
1 lemon, juiced and rind grated
1 pint blueberries
2 cups couscous

Bring juice to a boil in a sauce pan, add lemon rind and lemon juice. Add two cups of couscous, pouring in slowly and constantly to prevent lumping. Stir until couscous has absorbed juice and becomes thick; this will take about two or three minutes.

Add rinsed blueberries, allowing the heat to soften them; this takes about one minute. Some berries will burst, giving blue streaks to the cake. Rinse a glass or ceramic baking dish; pour the cake mix into the damp dish. Allow to cool and cut into squares. Glaze top with a fruit jelly.

HOLIDAY FRUIT CAKE*

*1 cup grated carrots
1 cup raisins
1/2 cup honey
1/4 cup chopped dates
1 tsp. cinnamon
1 tsp. allspice
1/2 tsp. nutmeg
1/4 tsp. ground cloves
1 3/4 cups water
1 1/2 cups whole wheat flour
1 tsp.. baking soda
1/2 cup bran*

Cook the carrots, raisins, dates, honey and spices in the water for 10 minutes. Cool. Mix together the flour, baking soda and bran. Add to the carrot mixture. Mix together well. Pour into non-stick loaf pan or 9" x 9" baking dish. Bake at 325 degrees for 45 minutes.

*THESE RECIPES ALTHOUGH VERY NATURAL ARE A GOOD EXAMPLE OF A "NATURAL ALTERNATIVE", BUT ARE POOR FOOD COMBINATIONS. THEY SHOULD NOT BE EATEN BY ANYONE BEYOND THE SOPHOMORE LEVEL AND RARELY BY ANYONE ELSE.

MAPLE SOY FROSTING

1 cup soy milk powder
1/2 cup maple syrup
2 Tbs. vanilla
3 Tbs. orange juice

Combine all ingredients and beat until smooth and creamy.

WHIPPED TOFU CREME TOPPING

1 14 oz. package soft tofu
5 Tbs. soy milk (plain or vanilla)
5 Tbs. maple syrup
1 Tbs. lemon juice
2 tsp. vanilla extract

Puree all ingredients in a blender until very smooth. Chill at least two hours before serving.

CAROB SAUCE

1 cup water
2 tsp. vanilla
2 Tbs. honey or natural liquid sweetener
2 Tbs. arrowroot powder or cornstarch
2 Tbs. roasted carob powder
1/2 tsp. powdered coffee substitute (optional)

Combine all ingredients. Bring to a boil, stirring constantly. Remove from heat when thickened.
Makes 1 1/4 cups.

"FRUITS"

FRUIT SQUARES

1 cup raisins
1 cup mixed dried fruit
1/2 cup almonds
2 Tbs. wheat germ
1/4 cup sunflower seeds, ground in blender
1/4 cup orange juice

Chop raisins, dried fruit and almonds. Combine with wheat germ, ground sunflower seeds, and enough juice to moisten. Press into an 8" baking pan lined with wax paper. Cover and let harden in the refrigerator for several hours. To serve, cut into squares with a knife dipped in hot water. Makes 8 - 1" candies

FROZEN BANANA CREME*

4 large frozen bananas
1 tsp. peanut butter

Cut bananas into chunks, and place in food process fitted with steel blade. Pulse until chopped. Add peanut butter and process until bananas are smooth and creamy. Serve immediately

*THIS RECIPE ALTHOUGH VERY NATURAL, IS A GOOD EXAMPLE OF A "NATURAL ALTERNATIVE" BUT A POOR FOOD COMBINATION. IT SHOULD NOT BE EATEN BY ANYONE BEYOND THE SOPHOMORE LEVEL AND RARELY BY ANYONE ELSE.

HOMEMADE APPLESAUCE

6 large apples
1 Tbs. lemon juice
2 Tbs. water
1/2 tsp. cinnamon
Maple syrup to taste (optional)

Peel, core, and cut up apples. Place them in a saucepan with lemon juice and water. Cover and cook about 20 minutes, or until apples are very soft. Stir in cinnamon and maple syrup, and blend until smooth.

FRUIT COMPOTE

1/2 cup dried apricots (about 4 - 6 oz.)
1/2 cup dried figs
1/2 cup raisins
3 cups apple juice or cider
1 tsp. vanilla
1 orange, juiced
Pinch of cinnamon, coriander, cardamon,
ginger, and nutmeg

Rinse the dried fruit in a strainer. Place in a sauce pot. Cover with the juice and bring to a boil, simmering for 30 minutes or longer until the fruit has swelled and is soft. Add the spices, vanilla and orange juice. Simmer for 5 to 10 minutes longer. The fruit should be plump, with a little liquid left in the pan.
Live Food Variation: Combine raw ingredients in a blender or food processor. Process until smooth.

FROZEN FRUIT SORBET

1 cup pineapple juice
1 frozen banana, sliced
1/2 - 1 cup frozen or fresh blueberries
or strawberries, sliced
2 cups frozen pineapple, sliced

Blend juice in blender at medium speed. While blender is running, add slices of frozen fruit through the feed opening in the blender lid.   Blend mixture until it has a "soft serve" consistency. Pour into serving dishes. Serve immediately or store in freezer for a short time before serving.

Serves 6

PIES/TARTS
*CAROB TOFU PIE**

Crust:
1 cup lightly roasted almonds
1/4 cup unsweetened, finely ground carob powder
1 tsp. vanilla extract : 1/8 tsp. almond extract
1 Tbs. liquid lecithin : 1 Tbs. maple syrup

Filling:
2 1/4 lbs. firm tofu
3/4 cup unsweetened, finely ground carob powder
2 1/2 tsp. vanilla extract : 3/4 tsp. almond extract
3/4 cup maple syrup : 2/3 cup cold water
2 tsp. powdered agar
Whipped soy cream (for garnish)

To make crust: Preheat oven to 375 degrees. With metal blade in place, add almonds to the work bowl of food processor. Pulse on and off until chopped medium-fine. Add carob powder, vanilla extract, almond extract, lecithin and maple syrup. Process only until well mixed. Press into bottom (not sides) of a well greased 9 1/2" spring form pan and bake for 8 minutes. Allow to cool completely before filling.

To make filling: Squeeze most of the moisture out of the tofu. Add to food processor. Process until smooth and creamy. Add carob powder, vanilla and almond extracts. Process until well mixed. In a small saucepan, combine maple syrup and water. Mix well. Sprinkle agar over the top. Let stand one minute to soften. bring to a boil, then reduce heat and continue boiling for 30 seconds. Cool for about 5 minutes. With machine running, slowly pour agar liquid into the tofu-carob mixture. Process a few seconds more to mix well. Pour on top of the crust and chill for 15 - 20 minutes.

See overleaf for variations

Variations: To filling add either peaches, apricots, or banana; reduce or eliminate carob powder, depending on your tastes. To Crust: Substitute raw cashews for almonds.

*THIS IS FOR THAT VERY SPECIAL OCCASION. BUT REMEMBER, IT IS STILL HEAVY AND NOT RECOMMENDED IF YOU RARELY EAT HEAVY FOODS.

RASPBERRY TART FILLING

2 cups apple raspberry juice
2/3 bar of agar-agar

Rinse agar-agar under running water for a few minutes until soft. It should have the texture of a wet sponge. Squeeze out excess liquid. Tear agar into little pieces and add to the juice. Bring juice and agar to a light boil; lower the flame, cover pan and simmer until agar is dissolved, approximately 5 - 7 minutes. Pour mixture into shallow bowl. Allow to cool, but not to set. Pour cooled filling into tart shell. Let filling set for 45 minutes to an hour in the refrigerator.

LEMON CUSTARD SAUCE

2 cups apple juice
3 Tbs. soy milk powder
1 lemon rind, grated
Juice from one lemon
3 Tbs. arrowroot powder (or)
2 Tbs. kuzu powder
1 tsp. pure vanilla extract

Whisk together soy milk powder and juice. Add lemon rind. Bring to light boil. Cover pan, lower flame and simmer for 5 - 7 minutes. Dissolve arrowroot or kuzu powder in lemon juice. Add to simmering liquid, stirring constantly until thick and custard like. Pour into shallow bowl and let cool. Serve over individual slices or raspberry tart. For a hot dessert, serve warm.

ORANGE CUSTARD FILLING

This is the same as the recipe for lemon custard sauce (above), but an orange is used instead of a lemon for the grated rind and juice, and 1/2 bar of agar is added to the soy milk and apple juice, giving the custard a thicker consistency. When adding agar, follow directions in raspberry filling recipe.

After you've let the orange custard cool, but not set, in a shallow bowl, pour it into a tart shell and allow to set for 45 minutes.

TOFU PARFAIT

2 cups soft tofu
1 cup fresh or frozen blueberries
2 small ripe bananas
2 Tbs. maple syrup
1/2 tsp. vanilla
Mint leaves for garnish

Blend all ingredients, except mint, and spoon into parfait or wine glasses. Chill one hour. Garnish with mint leaves.

ALMOND KANTEN MOUSSE

1 quart unsweetened apple juice
2 bars agar-agar torn into 1" pieces
1 Tbs. vanilla extract
1 Tbs. lemon juice
6 Tbs. almond butter
1/2 cup plain soy milk
1/4 cup slivered almonds, toasted
Fresh fruit

Combine the agar and apple juice in a large saucepan. Bring to a boil, then reduce to a simmer. Simmer, stirring until the agar is completely dissolved. Pour into a large bowl or pan. Refrigerate until the mixture is firm, about 1 hour.

Remove from refrigerator and puree in a blender, gradually adding the vanilla, lemon juice, almond butter and soy milk. Puree until the kanten is smooth. Return to refrigerator and chill at least an hour before serving.

Garnish with fresh fruit—any kind of berries or peeled and sliced soft fruit such as peaches or nectarines—add the toasted, slivered almonds.

Makes 6 servings.

CHARTS

Eating for Happiness *

DO NOT MIX more than four foods, from more than two classifications, at any one meal.

Use **ONE PROTEIN** food OR ONE STARCH food per meal.

OIL slow digestion.   Combines best with fruit and green vegetables;combines poorly with starch and protein.

TOMATO combines best with avocado and green vegetables

MELON (all kinds) should always be eaten alone.

AVOCADO combines best with acid fruit, sprouts and vegetables. Use in moderation.

WHEATGRASS should always be taken on an empty stomach. May mix with carrot and green vegetable and sprout juices

SEED CHEESE goes well with ripe sub-acid fruit, banana, leafy greens, sprouts, or alone.

Use **HONEY AND MOLASSES** on an empty stomach to prevent fermentation.

PEANUTS are high in protein, fat and starch and therefore difficult to digest.

Try eating one kind of **FRUIT** at a time or combining them according to type of seed: stone fruit(peach, nectarine, apricot, cherry), citrus fruit, core fruit (apples, pears) dried fruit, melon fruit. Papaya goes well with all sub-acid fruit as well as banana.

* Reprinted from: *Survival into the 21st Century Natural Planetary Healers Manual:* by Viktoras Kulvinskas, pp 267-69

What To Eat *

Organic live food is your best medicare, your ticket to prolonged youth. Eat natural food which appeals to you most.

Advance your diet according to the dictates of your body and the type of work you do.

Avoid all animal, processed, or cooked food, strong condiments and spices. Do not use the teeth to crush hard food. If hard to masticate, it is forbidden.

Grow your own food in your garden: vegetables, fruit, sprouts, 7 day greens. In a natural environment, eventually eat fruit only.

Be thrifty; eat what your own area can provide organically grown.

Eat no more than 16 ounces at a single meal. Never eat a large meal just before doing hard work. Before a difficult physical or mental task, center your energy; fast on juice or water.

When To Eat *

Eat only when hungry, after the previous meal is digested. No snacks between meals. Some individuals have within the digestive track three or more meals in a semi-digested, putrefactive state.

A day will not be wasted on a small(or no) breakfast.

Eat the biggest meal at noon when sun activity is strongest. Solar vibrations aid digestion. Eat a small meal before sunset for a longer night of fasting.

Never eat when in pain, emotionally upset, extremely tired or immediately after hard work.

Rest or relax after a meal for 45 minutes. For those with a delicate digestion, lie down for at least 10 minutes before a meal.

After retiring for the night, do not eat or drink.

How To Eat *

Begin with a name of God. Be grateful, ask for control in appetite. Bring a tranquil mind to meals. Do not argue or rush.

Enjoy the music of birds and brook, the silence of the sky. Enjoy your food.

Eat slowly and chew each mouthful thoroughly reducing it to fluid before swallowing. Breathe long and deep with each mouthful.

Do not drink (or eat) cold or hot (beyond 104 degrees) substances

No liquids with meals. Drink at least thirty minutes before or three hours after a meal.

Eat one food at a meal, or combine food correctly for best digestion. Eat juicy foods prior to concentrated foods. Eat raw foods before cooked foods. Stop eating before you feel full.

Reprinted from: *Survival into the 21st Century Natural Planetary Healers Manual:* by Viktoras Kulvinskas, pp 267-69

CHEMISTRY OF FOODS *

ACID ASH: All grain (except millet), all meat, butter, cream, eggs, cheese, animal fats, sea foods, most nuts, dry peas, dry beans, most oils, lentils, peanuts, hulled sesame.

MUCUS-INDUCING FOODS: All acid ash foods. All diary products. Sprouted grains, chick peas, lentils, seeds, nuts potato, yam. Slightly: Squash (Acorn, Butternut, Hubbard).

ALKALINE ASH: Most dried fruit, indoor greens, all grasses, dandelion, soybean sprouts, cucumber, almond, unhulled sesame, avocado, carrot, onion, tomato, peach, plum celery, fruit and most vegetables, olive oil, sprouts from most legumes.

ACID pH FRUIT: Currant, grapefruit, kumquat, lemon, lime, loganberry, loquat, orange, pineapple, pomegranate, strawberry, tamarind, tangerine, tangelo, tomato. When ripe, all fruits produce alkaline effect in the bloodstream. Overacid condition can be generated in the stomach regions, affecting your whole boy, from the intake of ascorbic acid(vitamin C), Nicotinic Acid, or any of the acidy vitamins, just as well as from eating unripe tomatoes, citrus or pineapple. Symptoms: dizziness, fainting, pressure on the eyes, headache, burning sensation in stomach, bleeding of the gums.

SUB-ACID FRUIT: Apple, apricot, blackberry, cactus fruit, cherimoya, cherry, elderberry, gooseberry, grape, guava, huckleberry, jujube, mango, nectarine, papaya, papaw, peach, pear, persimmon, plum, kiwi, raspberry, sapodilla, sapote.

MELON: Banana, cantaloupe, casaba, christmas, crenshaw, honeydew, persain, watermelon.

ACID FRUIT: Most berries pineapple and pomegranate leave the bloodstream more acid. When badly combined, or eaten in large quantity most food can leave the body more acid.

ALKALINE FRUIT: Citrus, tomatoes, most sweet fruit and those fruit listed sub-acid column leave the body more alkaline. Unripe, depleted soil sub-acid fruit are really acid.

SOAKED DRIED FRUIT such as figs, apples, apricots, peaches, dates and pears leave the body more alkaline. However, too much or too frequent or badly combined can cause fermentation and acidity in the bloodstream.

COLORED VEGETABLES: Beets, carrots, red cabbage, cauliflower, corn, eggplant, kohlrabi, parsnip, rutabaga, squashes, turnips, slightly mucus inducing.

COOKED VEGETABLES: During transition to raw foods all starchy food can be cooked. Eventually, lightly steam or bake the vegetables listed as fruit, green or colored. To slow down a rapid cleansing reaction slightly cooked vegetables may be used. Under such circumstances, you might want to blend together some raw and some cooked vegetables.

* Reprinted from: *Survival into the 21st Century Natural Planetary Healers Manual*:by Viktoras Kulvinskas pp. 267-69.

NATURAL LIVING CYCLES: 1 *

REJUVENATION+PURIFICATION = HARMONY IN BODY,
MIND AND SPIRIT

Rejuvenation=   *Vegetables (live and steamed) Chlorophyll, wheatgrass and Spirulina Rejuvenating herbs Fruits.*

Purification=   *Enemas, herbal laxatives and colonics Purification herbs.*

LEVELS OF MASTERY

1. Freshman   Organic chicken and fish (unshelled fish) baked or broiled.75% steamed vegetables, 25% raw vegetables. Whole grains, such as brown rich and bulgar wheat.

2. Sophomore   Soya meats, beans, peas, nuts, seeds and sprouts. 50% steamed vegetables, 50% raw vegetables. Whole grains, such as brown rich and bulgar wheat.

3. Junior   Sprouts(alfalfa, mung and others). 25% steamed vegetables, 75% raw vegetables. Lights grains, such as tabouli and couscous.

4. Senior   Live uncooked foods and sprouted proteins.100% raw diet of fresh fruits, vegetables, juices, nuts and seeds (pre-cooked, eaten in moderation)

5. Master   50% of diet consists of juices and herb teas. 50% of diet consists of fresh fruits and vegetables. No grains, nuts or seeds.

6. Ph.D.   A "Ph.D." purified diet would consist of 100% pure air and pure water. Alas, we must first cleanse the planet.

* Reprinted from: *"Heal Thyself with Health & Longevity"* by Queen Afua.

FOOD COMBINING FOR EASIER DIGESTION

PROTEIN		STARCHES
MEAT, EGGS, FISH, *(not recommended)* NUTS(MOST) FERMENTED SEED SAUCE SOYBEANS, COOKED OR SPROUTED SEED: SUNFLOWER, SESAME, PUMPKIN, CHIA.	P O O R	GRAINS COOKED OR SPROUTED MATURE BEANS AND PEAS, PEANUTS, POTATOES, BUTTERNUT, CHICK PEAS, COOKED OR SPROUTED, WINTER SQUASH: ACORN, HUBBARD.

GOOD   VEGETABLES   *GOOD*

POOR to FAIR   **POOR**

BUCKWHEAT LETTUCE	FRESH PEAS
LEAFY GREENS	JERSALEM ARTICHOKE
RADISH GREENS	PARSNIP (MILDY STARCHY)
SUNFLOWER GREENS	GREEN PEAS
WATERCRESS	SWEET PEPPER
WEED	SUMMER SQUASH
ASPARAGUS	TURNIP
BEET	CELERY
CARROT (MILDLY STARCHY)	

SPROUTS: MUNG, LENTIL, ALFALFA, FENUGREEK, RADISH, CUCUMBER (EAT ONLY WITH OTHER VEGETABLES)

POOR   *POOR*   *POOR*

ACID FRUIT

GRAPEFRUIT
LEMON
LIME
ORANGE
STRAWBERRIES
PINEAPPLES
POMEGRANATE
PLUMS(PRUNES)
BLACKBERRIES
TANGERINES
TANBERRIES
RASPBERRIES
KUMGUAT
UGLI

Sub-ACID FRUIT

APPLE
APPRICOT, KIWI
FRESH FLAG
GRAPE
MANGO
PAPAYA
PEAR PEACH
SWEET CHERRY
BLUEBERRIES
NECTARINE

SWEET FRUIT

BANANA
DATE
DRIED FLAG
DRIED FRUIT
RAISIN
PERSIMON

BAD COMBINATION

PROTEIN AND STARCH
OIL AND STARCH
FRUIT AND STARCH

POOR COMBINATION

PROTEIN AND ACID FRUIT
LEAFY GREENS AND ACID FRUIT
LEAFY GREENS AND SUBACID FRUIT

GOOD COMBINATION

PROTEIN AND LEAFY GREENS STARCH AND VEGETABLES
OIL AND ACID SUBACID FRUIT
OIL AND LEAFY GREENS

NATURAL VITAMIN SUPPLEMENTS *

Calcium Forms   Oatstraw & Comfrey Herbs, Sprouts, Carrots, Green Leafy Vegetables, Nut Milk, Soy Milk

Vitamin A/D   Carrots

Vitamin B   Yeast, Bee Pollen

Vitamin C   Rosehips Herb Tea

Vitamin E   Alfalfa, Wheatgrass

Minerals   Kelp, Other Sea Plants, Spirulina, Blue/Green Manna

Fun Foods   Freshly prepared Popcorn, Brown Rice Cakes, Dried Fruits (ie., Banana Chips, Pineapple, Apricots, Raisins), Banana Custard, Frozen Fruit Juice (instead of ices), Chilled Fruit (ie., Grapes, Oranges, Baked Apples).

* Reprinted from: *"Heal Thyself with Health & Longevity"* by Queen Afua.

"VEGETARIAN SUBSTITUTES"

Dairy and Egg Substitutes

Milk   Soy milk, nut milk, rice or oat milk, banana milk

Yogurt   Soy yogurt

Cheese   Mashed soft tofu small amounts of miso or tamari to add saltiness

Butter   Soy margarine, vegetable oil (7/8 cup oil for 1 cup butter), nut butters, fruit butters or preserves to spread on bread

Sour Cream   Blend soft tofu with lemon juice and herbs

Eggs To replace 1 egg in baked goods:
1 tsp. commercial egg replacer, plus 2 Tbs. water;
1 Tbs. arrowroot, 1 Tbs soyflour, plus 2 Tbs. water;
2 Tbs. flour, 1/2 Tbs. vegetable shortening, 1/2 tsp.
baking powder, plus 2 Tbs. water;
1/8 lb. tofu blended with the liquid in the recipe you are
using; 1/2 large banana, mashed

To replace eggs in casseroles, mashed avocado, tahini and nut
burgers and loaves butters, or rolled oats

"SWEET SUBSTITUTES"

These measurements are substitutions for 1 cup of sugar.

Natural Sweetener	Substitute	Liquid Reduction
Honey	3/4 cup	1/8 cup
Maple Syrup	3/4 cup	1/8 cup
Maple Granules	1 cup	-
Molasses	1/2 cup	-
Date Sugar	1 cup	-
Barley Malt	1 1/2 cup	slightly
Fruit Juice Concentrate	1 1/2 cup	1/8 cup

"FOOD ALTERNATIVES"

LOW VIBRATION FOODS	HIGH VIBRATION FOODS
	(Eat Between Noon & 4 P.M. Only!)
Cow's Milk	Soy Milk, Nut Milk, Goats Milk, Kafir, Mother's Milk
Ice Cream	Soy Ice Cream
Cheese	Rennetless Unsalted Cheese or Grated Tofu
Margarine	Soya Margarine
Dannon Yogurt	Brown Cow Yogurt (Best Not To Eat!)

Eggs	Organic Eggs (Try To Avoid!)
White Bread	Whole Wheat or Cracked Wheat Bread
White Macaroni	Whole Wheat Macaroni
White Rice	Brown Rice
White Flour	Whole Wheat Flour or Barley Flour
Other Grains	Millet, Couscous, Bulgur
Pancakes	Buckwheat, Whole Wheat, Bran or Flax Seed Pancakes
Grits	Soy Grits, Barley Grits
Oil	Cold Pressed Olive Oil
Commercial Cereal (ie., Corn Flakes or Sugar Pops)	Whole Oats, Granola
Meat, Poultry, fish	Sprouts, Tofu, Seeds, Nuts, Miso, Beans
Corn Starch	Arrow Root Powder
White Sugar	Raw Honey, Maple Syrup, Black Strap Molasses, Fructose
Canned or Frozen Vegetables	Fresh Vegetables (Steamed or Raw)
Soda	Fresh Juice, Mineral Water or Pierre Water
Vinegar	Apple Cider Vinegar
Salt	Sea Salt, Kelp, Dulse
Chocolate	Carob
Gelatin	Agar-Agar
Water	Distilled or Spring Water
Bottled or Canned Fruit Juice	Fresh Squeezed/Pressed Fruit Juice
Jiffy Peanut Butter	Fresh Unsweetened Peanut Butter

Reprinted from: "*Heal Thyself with Health & Longevity*" by Queen Afua

Note

If you have a high percentage of live food in your diet or are beyond a "*sophomore level*" in Queen Afua's Natural Living Program many of the heavier recipes which contain tofu, nuts rice, gravies or pasta may be too heavy and should not be eaten

ABOUT THE AUTHOR

Diane Ciccone- Mother, healer and lawyer has been on the path of purification for over twenty years. She believes in the purification of the body temple through the art of fasting and the natural living process. She has studied with Dr. John E. Moore, the Rev. Philip Valentine and is currently studying with Queen Afua.

Diane is a graduate of Colgate University and Hofstra School of Law. She is in private practice in New York.

When Diane is not working or studying, she can be found in her kitchen cooking new and healthy recipes for her husband and daughter.

● ● ● ● ● ● ●

People often ask me why I'm a vegetarian. I tell the story my father tells, that as a little girl I would sit at the dinner table, sometimes until bedtime, because I kept chewing the meat and didn't want to swallow. As a teen, I read Adele Davis', "*Eat Right to Live*", Upton Sinclair's "*Slaughterhouse*", and "*The Autobiography of Malcolm X*". Those three books gave me the resolve and commitment to act out my belief that eating meat was not only unnecessary to good health, but also detrimental. Becoming a vegetarian in 1970 wasn't fashionable or acceptable. I was ill prepared for the daily challenges to learn how to eat differently than those all around me. This book is important to me because it gives you simple recipes to insure a good wholesome diet.

In closing, I hope this book will be a guide in your quest for a healthier and lighter diet. As you make this journey remember that old adage " you eat what you are and are what you eat."

Diane Ciccone